SIBELIUS: A CLOSE-UP

Sibelius: A Close-Up

by

Bengt de Törne

Boston
Houghton Mifflin Company
1938

Printed in Great Britain

Dedicated to my friend
TANCRED BORENIUS
with whom the idea of this book originated

PREFACE

Sibelius is not in favour of long introductions (on this point the reader may consult page 93) and I shall not burden the present book with one.

I feel it however incumbent on myself, since an egotistical note is inevitable in a study of this kind, to stress the fact that my whole ambition has been to play Boswell to the Dr. Johnson of Sibelius.

I must not omit to record my gratitude to Miss Clarissa Borenius, Mr. Sacheverell Sitwell and Mr. Cecil Gray, whose kindness and help have meant so much to me.

B. DE T.

London, February 1937

NOTE

The bracketed numbers in the text refer to Musical Examples which will be found at the end of the book.

I

Many years ago Sibelius went to a bank in order to present a bill of exchange. The man in the office took the document that the master handed him and looked at it rather doubtfully. After a moment he shrugged his shoulders and said: 'I am afraid, Sir, that we don't know this name!'

At that time Sibelius was already considered one of the world's masters. Definite consecration, however, was not given him until his fiftieth birthday. The whole of Finland celebrated this great event, and during the entire winter Sibelius' works were performed.

Among the numerous adepts of Finland at that time there was a young composer, who had nothing more to boast of in life than a quite recent diploma from the Conservatoire of Helsingfors in his pocket and an equally recent piano quintette under his arm. This quite insignificant person is mentioned here, as he has now the honour of telling the public all about his acquaintance with Sibelius.

There was also in Finland at that time a great conductor called Robert Kajanus, who had seen my quintette; and one day he asked me to come to a rehearsal of a symphony concert. He was to give a performance of Sibelius' Fourth symphony, and the master had promised to come round towards the end of the rehearsal in order to give some hints as to the interpretation of this work. Kajanus thought this might be an excellent opportunity of introducing me to Sibelius. The plan, however, was upset by the master who suddenly entered the hall and made straight for me, leaving me no chance of running away and hiding in a dark corner, as I cordially wished to do.

He paid no attention to the orchestra for the moment, but looked at me intently. His clear eyes were full of sadness and kindliness, whereas his closed mouth expressed power, strength and energy. After a while he asked: 'Who are you?' I stammered my name, feeling that a man from China would have pronounced it far more accurately. Having heard it he shook hands with me very cordially and told me that he had known my father. 'And now,' he said,

12

'let us sit down. I am glad to listen to my Fourth symphony in your company.'

It was from this moment that the mysteries of modern orchestration began to be unveiled to me. Sibelius spoke nearly all the time in a low voice, explaining details and shades of the symphony and pointing out some of its outlines. He also discussed various ways of rendering it and compared the interpretations he had heard in different places. No doubt many conductors would have given the world to be present at this rehearsal.

Without knowing it Sibelius gave a most fascinating exposé of his views on the rendering of his own work. It was all the more interesting as he had before him one of the greatest interpreters of his inspirations. Kajanus was the man who first discovered and understood the genius of Sibelius. With unique unselfishness and modesty he devoted a large part of his long and brilliant career as a conductor to performances of his friend's work, although he was himself a composer of great distinction. Nobody has ever grasped the character of the master's work more profoundly and intimately than Kajanus, the creator of the world-wide Sibelius tradition. When studying Sibelius' scores he used to discuss them with the author himself, asking for his advice in order to avoid any uncertainty. And when Sibelius was to

13

give a first performance of a new and unknown work of his, Kajanus at once tried to discover his friend's intentions as to the rendering of it. This was no easy task, for Sibelius never allowed anybody to be present when rehearsing with the orchestra. Kajanus used therefore to ask the attendant to let him into the gallery long before Sibelius arrived. He remained there unseen for the whole rehearsal and only emerged from his recess when he was quite sure that Sibelius had already left. One day, however, he came down the staircase to find Sibelius in the entrance-hall. They eyed one another for a while, and then Sibelius reproached his friend for using such stratagems. But his face broke into a smile when Kajanus explained the matter to him. 'You know', Kajanus said, 'that I am to conduct it after you. I want my interpretation to conform as far as possible to your own intentions, and this is the only means of getting first-hand information.'

While we listened to Kajanus rehearsing his Fourth symphony, Sibelius first of all pointed out to me his friend's familiarity with the subject. It was an acquaintance with the score, he said, which went far beyond even the most accurate knowledge of all his notes. He explained his idea, adding that a conductor should not give a performance of a work after a rushed, although energetic study of the score. On

14

the contrary, the score should gradually penetrate his mind by means of a patient psychological experience. 'Kajanus has grasped the spirit of my symphony,' he said. But he made me understand that according to him even a man with Kajanus' great musical intelligence and fine artistic intuition would reach absolute perfection only after long and repeated study of the score.

And so it was. Even in his last years you would see Kajanus poring over Sibelius' scores before performing his work. 'You can never know the score too well,' he explained. One day, years ago, I said to him, that I supposed he knew every single note of Sibelius' symphonic work; and upon his answering in the affirmative I asked him if he had never felt tempted to conduct some of his friend's masterpieces by heart. 'You know,' he replied, 'I once gave Sibelius' First symphony without the score. Everything went very well, and I even received congratulations on the performance. But afterwards I was struck with remorse, thinking that I might have omitted some shades, even if nobody had noticed. And thereupon I promised myself never to conduct anything by heart again.' No doubt this scrupulousness was consistent with Sibelius' own view on the rendering of his work, but the master would never have suggested such rigorous discipline as Kajanus imposed on himself.

15

I remembered these words of Kajanus, showing his extreme modesty. Sibelius praised his friend for the way he prepared the performance of his Fourth symphony.

Having insisted on the importance of a profound knowledge of the score, Sibelius turned to the second main requirement of a conductor: homogeneity and unity of conception. 'You see how Kajanus builds up my symphony,' he proceeded. 'He actually makes you feel the construction of the work like a huge building.' You felt that these words meant the highest praise he could bestow upon a conductor. He emphasized the necessity of balancing the masses against each other and the importance of defining the outlines. In so doing the conductor would always be sure of rendering the intentions of the composer instead of betraying them. As long as he kept in mind the main construction of the work he was performing, he would never lose his sense of proportion or give too much importance to one single detail, however beautiful in itself. Once this general idea was accepted, attention could be concentrated on the different episodes, epic, lyric or dramatic, without sacrifice of unity.

On another occasion Sibelius expressed the same idea although in a different way. Kajanus conducted the *Eroica* at a symphony concert in Helsinfgors. It was an exceptionally fine performance, every detail, however carefully worked out, being subordinate to the grand architectural conception. After the concert I went to see Kajanus. On entering the artists' room I found him being warmly congratulated by Sibelius. I waited for a moment at the door. Suddenly Sibelius discovered me, made straight for me, took my hand and said enthusiastically: 'Did you understand *how* wonderful it was?' He then emphasized the monumental unity of the interpretation and concluded: 'I wish all the young people had heard it!'

At the rehearsal of his Fourth symphony Sibelius also discussed different details of the interpretation. There was above all one thought which recurred in his exposé like a leitmotiv in a Wagnerian drama: the conductor was under no circumstances to indulge in exaggeration. He told me how profoundly he appreciated the strong and noble sense of style which dominated Kajanus' interpretation of his music. Given this, Sibelius would freely admit the most elaborate working out of shades. He pointed out to me that in Kajanus' performance of his symphony you never lost sight of the main outlines of the score in spite of the most exquisite rendering of its minor details.

Sibelius is very sensitive to anything that may

happen at a rehearsal, whether an accident or a particularly brilliant reply of some instrument.

One day when Kajanus was rehearsing Sibelius' Third symphony he had asked the master to come round and discuss certain points in the score. I sat opposite the orchestra. Sibelius entered the hall and took a seat next to the main entrance. For some time everything went well and Sibelius obviously enjoyed listening to the orchestra. He gazed at the floor and seemed entirely absorbed in his own music. But suddenly the first trumpet blundered. Sibelius at once raised his head as if awakened from an enchanting dream. He gave the orchestra a startled look, then rose to his feet and made for the door, trying to leave the room unobserved. Neither Kajanus nor the musicians noticed him and the rehearsal went on undisturbed. But no sooner had the last notes of the finale died away, than Kajanus turned towards the door and asked for Sibelius. Seeing that nobody was there, he looked at me. 'Where is Sibelius?' Upon my telling him that the master had left, he at first seemed rather surprised, then smiled and said: 'I ought to have foreseen it, knowing him as I do. That trumpet was too much for him. He couldn't stand it, but on the other hand he didn't want to hurt the poor man's feelings by telling him, so he simply left.' Kajanus laughed, and added: 'This reminds me of

18

something similar that happened many years ago. Sibelius came to hear me rehearsing his Second symphony. Unfortunately I had no third trumpet that day, the man being laid up with flu. For a while Sibelius tried to listen, becoming more and more restless. Then suddenly he got up, came over to me and said: "Will you kindly excuse my leaving at once? I can only hear the trumpet which isn't there, and I can't stand it any longer!" '

Sibelius gladly notices every good performance at rehearsals. Sometimes it is an oboe or a horn, sometimes a stringed instrument which attracts his attention. One day when rehearsing with the orchestra he was struck by the great accuracy of the principal second violin. For a while he listened chiefly to him, although conducting the whole ensemble. He could not help looking more and more intently at the man who gave him such pleasure. The poor musician felt rather uneasy, seeing the master's eye fixed on him, and thought there was something wrong with his playing. He did not feel any happier when Sibelius interrupted the orchestra and pointed him out with his baton to all the other players. But to his astonishment he heard the master saying: 'You play very well indeed! I just wanted to interrupt the orchestra to tell you that.' After a moment of general cheerfulness the rehearsal continued.

The day I first met Sibelius he remained with me right up to the end of the rehearsal. After the finale he got up, went to Kajanus and shook hands with him. The conductor modestly asked Sibelius to criticize his interpretation of the symphony. 'I've nothing to say,' Sibelius replied, 'except that I am perfectly satisfied with your rendering of it.' But Kajanus would not accept this answer. 'I suggested that you should come round', he said, 'because I wanted you to help me. And I ask it as a favour: do let me have your criticisms.' Sibelius repeated his assurances, whereupon Kajanus opened the score to discuss some of its indications with the master. He always did this when opportunity arose, in his efforts to complete or even correct the indications of the printed edition. Once he spoke to me about *The Oceanides*. 'It has been published,' he said, 'but unfortunately there are many errors in the score. I went through it with Sibelius one day and found that its indications of tempi, shades and so on are quite wrong.'

The two friends remained poring over the score of the Fourth symphony for a while. I saw Kajanus turning over the pages and heard him asking for advice as to the rendering of different passages.

Meanwhile all the musicians had left the hall. Kajanus shut the score and, discovering me, said to

Sibelius: 'I would like you to meet a young composer. May I introduce to you——' 'You needn't bother,' Sibelius interrupted. 'We have got to know each other during my Fourth symphony, and I am sure our acquaintance will continue.' And he shook hands with me again. 'I think,' Kajanus said, 'that Monsieur de Törne would like to submit something to you.' Sibelius asked whether it was a composition, and, on my confessing this, he remarked: 'Do you know, I have had some unfortunate experiences with young composers showing me their scores.' His look expressed the utmost melancholy. 'No sooner do I say anything about their compositions than they lose their tempers. And they have no difficulty in persuading me that they are perfectly right, whereas I am completely wrong to venture even the feeblest criticism of their work.' Kajanus now replied that he thought he could so far guarantee the placidity of my temperament, and I chimed in protesting that I only hoped for very severe criticism. At that, Sibelius opened his arms and smiled broadly. 'If so,' he said, 'you are *my* man. Depend on it, you will get the criticism in so many words!'

Thereupon he shook hands with me, asking me to come and see him one day of the following week at the hotel where he usually put up when he came in to Helsingfors from the country.

II

Next week I took myself and my quintette to the hotel. I knew that Kajanus had spoken to Sibelius about it, and the tiny little score felt like heavy lead in my hand. On entering the master's room I at first saw nothing but a greyish blue cloud, which bore the aroma of strong and good cigars. At the other end of the room I dimly discerned the outlines of a man; and as he rose to his feet and approached me, I gradually recognized the master.

'This is a very great pleasure,' he said, shaking hands. I apologized for trespassing upon his valuable time. 'No, no, no, don't talk like that! I never flatter anybody and I never use conventional phrases: it *is* a pleasure for me to receive you here. Now, where are you going to sit? There, for instance!' He showed me a chair and I sat down. Suddenly he exclaimed:

'No, not that chair! It isn't good enough: this is the best one, do sit down here.'

I had to obey for a moment, and then made an attempt to leave him the chair, but was gently pushed back. 'You are my guest,' he explained, '*my honoured guest.*' He laid stress on these last words. 'May I offer you a cigar?' I told him that I did not smoke, and he exclaimed: 'How I envy you! With me it is a vice: I have become the slave of my cigars. I hope you will permit me to smoke. Oh! I see that you have brought something with you, that was nice of you! Is it your quintette? Can I have a look at it?'

I handed him the score and tried to explain that it must be regarded merely as the work of a pupil, the result of purely theoretical studies.

Sibelius opened the score and read the first pages. I tried to catch the expression of his face, but could not decide whether he looked censorious or only absorbed in the indifferent piece of music he was reading. Suddenly he said: 'You must not worry about your future,' and after a while there came other remarks to the same effect. They only made me feel more uneasy. Eventually I timidly tried to say that I was afraid he was far too indulgent. He looked up at me. 'You don't suppose that I judge you from this score, do you?' he said. 'I am quite aware that you have only just left the Conservatoire. But I can see

24

from this quintette what you will do in ten or twenty years' time.'

I told him that I was only too conscious of all the great difficulties to be overcome by any young composer taking his task seriously. As for myself, I added, I felt convinced that it would take me many years to discover myself and find my own way. 'You know,' he remarked, 'it is often a very good sign if an artist is slow in unveiling his temperament and developing his own personal style. It means that he has got the epic, the symphonic strain. Besides, we are both northerners, which means that we don't find ourselves at once.'

He then took up the score again and read it through right to the end. Every now and then he mentioned some feature of it, but always in the most indulgent way. I felt rather disappointed, for I had expected something quite different. At last I ventured to remind him of his promise to give me a severe criticism. 'Yes,' he said, 'and here is my verdict. I see your future clearly and you have a friend in me.'

I knew that Sibelius never accepted pupils. But his last words gave me the courage to ask him, whether he would grant me the great privilege of studying orchestration with him.

'Of course I will,' he answered unhesitatingly.

'But, you know, I don't teach at all and I cannot give you ordinary lessons.' And with that modesty which is so characteristic of him he added: 'Besides, I don't know whether I am a good teacher or not; I think the better the composer, the worse the teacher. Anyhow, I might be able to give you some hints which you wouldn't find in books about orchestration; and I shall give you the secrets of my long experience.'

As I tried to thank him for his generous suggestion, he said: 'Now, since you have become my pupil, I must see into your mind, because I can't be expected to teach you something if I don't know you thoroughly. Look at me. No, not that way; straight into my eyes.'

He suddenly grew silent, his face assuming a serious, almost severe expression, and as he sat motionless I felt his keen scrutiny right through my head. Presently there came words, pronounced quite slowly and in a low voice. He told me all about myself and my life. It was the clearest and most perspicacious psychological analysis I had ever heard.

You might well have believed that he had thought it over for a long time, so logical was the demonstration as a whole, so irrefutable seemed its different arguments. His starting-point was the supposition

26

that the mentality of young artists is as a rule very complicated; he tried to point out the principal ingredients, their intrinsic virtues and influences one upon another. Next he described different types of artists, and finally turned to my particular case. With an infinite subtlety he explained to me the successive phases of my mental development. He dwelt on my present state of mind. He then sketched the consequences of it to indicate my future possibilities. I sat there fascinated, almost spellbound by his amazing intuition. Still, I could not help feeling that his general characterization was far too benevolent. He finished his analysis by harking back to the features revealed by him when perusing my quintette. I told him that I felt quite overwhelmed, and that there was nothing to add. He said, with a smile: 'I have seen so much of life.'

Then his voice changed in tone as he told me that he wanted to give me some good advice. 'Never pay any attention to what critics say,' he proceeded, and expatiated on this theme. When I ventured to put in the remark that their articles might sometimes be of great importance, he cut me short. 'Remember,' he said, 'a statue has never been set up in honour of a critic!'

I rose to my feet and thanked him for this never-to-be-forgotten afternoon, but was interrupted at once. 'You must not thank me; it is I who wish to thank you for the pleasure you gave me by coming to see me. Do come again next week! We will have our introductory lesson then. That will be very nice, and I am looking forward to it.' He then followed me to the door and, opening it, said: 'You know, you can always rely on me, and you have a friend in me.'

III

The next time I went to see Sibelius I was received at once as an old and intimate friend.

'We'll discuss orchestration,' he began. 'I am myself a man of the orchestra. You must judge me from my orchestral works.' And he added half jokingly: 'I write piano pieces in my free moments.' Then, quite seriously again: 'As a matter of fact the piano does not interest me; it cannot sing. And I never go to piano recitals except when they are given by real geniuses, like my friend Busoni.

'You know, I could talk to you about the orchestra every day for a year, without exhausting the subject. There are different ways of treating this vast ensemble. Everybody can learn the average conservatoire orchestration, but that is still very far from real instrumentation. It has become a fashion of late

29

to make the orchestra purvey for the successful tradesman and earn his applause.'

This saying, however facetious in form, expresses a profound and serious conviction of Sibelius. In our conversations he would never admit the claims of the more popular aesthetic currents. His own music is essentially esoteric. But such is the magic of his inspiration, he has found friends and admirers everywhere. Like all great art Sibelius' music can be enjoyed by everybody, although it will perhaps be reserved for comparatively few to reach a higher degree of comprehension of his greater symphonic works.

He went on to say that he had never stopped to ask whether he infringed the orthodox rules of good orchestration. On the other hand, he had not abandoned the main road expressly to create sensation, but only when it had suited his purpose. This statement expresses his entire artistic creed: innovation must come from within and not be aimed at deliberately. He finished this part of his exposition by saying: 'You know, I am not legitimately married to the orchestra; I am its lover.'

After these remarks he attacked the subject itself. 'The orchestra, you see, is a huge and wonderful instrument that has got everything—except the pedal. You must always bear this in mind. You see, if you don't create an artificial pedal for your

30

orchestration there will be holes in it, and some passages will sound ragged. Many composers, even great geniuses, either never discovered this or entirely forgot it—Liszt, for instance. He is too pianistic in his orchestral works and too orchestral in his piano pieces. While he was writing his scores he sat at the piano, pressing the pedal, and everything sounded perfect. But in the orchestra there was no substitute for the pedal accommodating enough to avoid the danger of sudden emptiness, and fuse all the different and sometimes incompatible groups of sounds.

'If a modern orchestration does not sound well it generally means the same fault, or a far too heavy agglomeration of instruments, especially in the lower register.'

Sibelius now told me that in his opinion there was another pedal question, quite apart from the first. He added that he expected to come back to it later on, when he had discussed some means of avoiding the holes and obtaining the effect of the pedal, that is to say, the continuation of sonority when passing from one group of colours to another. 'Mind you, this only refers to the wind instruments,' he pointed out. 'I always fit in some second violins or violas in the medium register, which has no characteristic colour of its own. You practically only hear the wind, but the continuity is there.'

Sibelius' own scores offer many interesting examples of this technique. The andante of his Second symphony is perhaps one of the most instructive. Among other means of creating pedal he would suggest quavers on the kettle-drums, and pizzicati. But, unlike his use of violins and violas, these methods introduce a new colour of their own.

None of the great classical works on orchestration deals with this question of the pedal. It is true that some of their indications occasionally point towards a solution; and by experience most composers have from time to time been induced to adopt methods analogous to those recommended by Sibelius. But it is one of the great merits of Sibelius to have understood the question so clearly and to have applied the solution of the problem so consistently in his own work. The amazing sonority of his orchestration is certainly in a large measure due to this pedal technique. In this, as in many other examples of his method, what is purely technical also expresses the attitude towards life and the artistic philosophy of the master. The great unity and homogeneity of colour thus obtained, in spite of the infinite variety of timbre, derive from a symphonic, that is to say, epic conception of life. I shall return to this question in a later chapter devoted entirely to Sibelius' views on the symphonic form.

Many composers nowadays increase the hardness of their harmonic tissue, the coincidence of discordant notes, by their orchestral writing. Of Sibelius the reverse is true; the somewhat strange impression of some of his harmonic anticipations is always softened by the orchestration. (1)

Sibelius also discussed the second part of the pedal problem in modern orchestration, which again has two aspects. The first corresponds to the effect obtained at the piano when pressing the pedal, striking a fortissimo harmony and letting it die away. In the orchestra an analogous effect may be obtained by giving the beginning of the chord to trumpets, trombones, horns and wood-wind, all fortissimo. A diminuendo follows and gradually the stronger instruments are dropped, leaving only horns and clarinets, flutes or bassoons to finish their diminuendo on the subtlest pianissimo. 'Thus you will achieve a thing of ideal beauty,' Sibelius said. Raising his arms and opening them, to describe it plastically, he added: 'It will be like a thought, born under a heavy sky and trying to reach purer regions.'

He then dealt with the second aspect of the question. Suppose you successively strike groups of notes on different octaves of the keyboard, all belonging to the same chord, at the same time pressing the pedal: you will obtain an effect well known to all

c 33 s.a.c.

piano players. The composer, who wishes to achieve an analogous effect with the orchestra, should introduce one by one the groups of instruments corresponding to the different octaves of the piano. He may then interrupt them gradually. But before excluding one group he should always introduce the next, this being the secret of the pedal effect. Sibelius' work offers many instances of this method. The famous opening bars of *The Swan of Tuonela* (2) and the beginning of *Tapiola* (3) are especially striking.

Having pointed out one deficiency of the orchestra, that it has no pedal, Sibelius turned to another: that the trio of trombones, although the most powerful part of the modern orchestra, has no proper foundation. 'You know as well as I do', he proceeded, 'that the timbre of the tuba simply does not fit in with that of the trombones. And if for purely dynamic reasons you think you must let the tuba support the trombones, do try to make it as unobtrusive as possible by adding other instruments like the bassoons, double basses and so on.' It may be added that one of the means employed by Sibelius is a strong quaver on the kettle-drums. The end of the first movement of the First symphony offers a fine example of this method. (4) Sibelius particularly recommended another technical expedient: a bass-clarinet supporting the tuba in unison. 'Long experience has taught me that this is a very happy solution of the problem,' he added. 'Only, it is not available in a grand fortissimo.' This statement of Sibelius will surprise connoisseurs of the master's music; which only makes it the more interesting. The fact is that very few of Sibelius' scores contain a bass-clarinet part. It may therefore be assumed that the 'experience' he mentioned refers to works which have not yet been printed or performed.

Sibelius continued: 'Personally, I feel convinced that a composer can do without the tuba. I do not like this instrument; to my mind it is far too heavy —what the Germans call *schwerfällig*. In my later works I have eliminated it, as, for instance, in my Fourth symphony, through which we met. There is always a way of building up a fortissimo without a tuba.' (5)

His compositions support these statements. Whereas the tuba plays a very important part in the first two symphonies, it does not appear in any of the subsequent scores.

From the tuba Sibelius turned to the trio of trombones. He told me that he strongly disapproved of the lavish way it has been employed in some modern scores. He particularly recommended me always to keep it as an entity. In his own work he very rarely breaks the unity, and then only to obtain some particular effect, as in one passage of the famous finale of the Second symphony. (6) This is exceptional. As a rule, the unity of the trio is preserved in Sibelius' compositions, although a distinct evolution within this entity can be traced. In the earlier works the three trombones form a compact, homophonous mass, (7) whereas the later scores show an elaborate polyphony, which allows each trombone the fullest independence. (8)

Wagner's music has meant practically nothing to Sibelius; the influence of his orchestral idiom, even less. Yet as regards their treatment of the tuba and the trio of trombones an interesting parallel can be noticed in the evolution of both. In Wagner's earlier works, as in Sibelius' first two symphonies, the tuba plays a very important part. The 'Faust' overture opens on a theme given by this instrument and the prelude to *Tannhäuser* contains a climax assigned to it—a passage no longer quite satisfactory to musical ears. The famous song to the evening star is partly accompanied by the trombones, courageously supported by the tuba, while broken chords are given by the harp, that inevitable accessory to any self-respecting moonlight scene. In Wagner's later works we do not find such amalgamations.

Every concert-goer will have noticed Wagner's great predilection for the trombones. He never breaks the unity of this trio, but the *Mastersingers* contains passages where the compact, homophonous mass of the earlier scores is transformed into an elaborate polyphonic ensemble of three individuals. This evolution has a counterpart in Sibelius' work— the Seventh symphony, for instance, compared to the master's early manner.

Having discussed the problem of tuba and trombones, Sibelius made some general aesthetic remarks on the orchestra. 'Always remember,' he said, 'that even the best orchestration ceases to be good as soon as it becomes the aim of the composer instead of remaining a means.

'You must never write anything without knowing exactly how it will sound. By employing unusual registers of instruments you can sometimes obtain quite new and interesting colours. But this does not mean that you should go in for extravagant experiments, as unfortunately so many people seem to do nowadays. Let us take an instance. Suppose you wish to write a third and let the lowest tone of the flute play its fundamental note: you can very well give the upper note to the tuba. But, whereas in this case the flute has a very striking colour, the top register of the tuba is completely devoid of any trace of

37

character and just sounds like a bad and weak horn. So the only result will be that your invention looks "interesting" in the score.'

Sibelius lives up to the opinions he professes. The rich colour of his scores is obtained by the simplest means. It is rare for him to resort to unusual registers, or to passages which could be labelled as contrary to the generally admitted character of the instruments. And when he does, it is a psychological and artistic necessity. The low flutes, oboes and clarinets, for instance, which can sometimes be heard in his works, never remain merely experimental but always evoke a strange, remote and fascinating atmosphere. (9) And the grace-notes of the horns in the Fifth and Seventh symphonies— quite exceptional writing for these instruments— seem to bring us messages from a weird, unknown world. (10)

Sibelius concluded his general remarks by saying: 'Next time we will have our first regular lesson.' He thereupon suggested that I should score the first movement of Beethoven's Waldstein sonata for full symphonic orchestra and then show it to him. I tried to protest, telling him that I was only a beginner. 'So am I,' he answered, 'and so are we all, or at least we should feel we are. But perhaps I could help you on your way.' He lowered his head, putting

38

his fingers in his ears, and there came over his face an expression of intense inward listening. Presently he said: 'You must start with one pizzicato for the double basses and then let the second violins, the violas and the violoncellos play the whole first bar staccato. At the second bar you will make the bassoons join them, but legato. And give the little treble chirp to the first violins and not to the flute. I leave the rest to you!'

Feeling that the task was far too heavy for me, I thought, as Ibsen did, on seeing one of his own plays: 'How the deuce is this going to end?' But when I expressed my doubts as to the result Sibelius only encouraged me by saying: 'You must jump into the water and then try to swim.'

He told me that next time he wanted me to come to lunch with him and his wife at their country house. 'I think that will be the best way of beginning our first lesson,' he explained. To which, on my thanking him, he added these important words: 'And I am going to prepare the salad myself!'

IV

It was on a fine day in June that I went to see
Sibelius in the country. After a drive through
sunny fields, the car turned suddenly to the left,
leaving the highway for the private road leading to
the master's home. As we came to the edge of a
wood I discovered a white house with a high, steep
roof, charmingly situated on a hill and sheltered by
transparent pale birches and sombre firs. On the
slope in front of the house there were glimpses of
flowers between the trunks of the trees and farther
down at the foot of the hill a tennis court lay sur-
rounded by green meadows. A winding road led up
to the main entrance.

I rang the bell and was shown into the drawing-
room. Opposite the entrance there was a window,
which opened on a very attractive view: across the
waving cornfields you saw the glittering surface of

one of those famous Finnish lakes, which used to be one thousand when we were young, but whose number, with the progress of journalism, tourism and other glorious achievements of modern civilization, has been officially increased to sixty thousand. A grand piano, some bookshelves and white chairs gave the room an inviting character. The walls were covered with paintings by our best Finnish artists, given to Sibelius as marks of friendship and admiration. Among them there was an old portrait of the master by his friend Gallén-Kallela. You could tell from the look of the young man on the canvas that he would make the world listen to him.

After a while I heard a chair being moved on the upper floor and then steps coming down the staircase. The door opened and Sibelius entered the room. 'You must excuse me,' he said. 'I did not hear you coming. Have you been waiting long?' I told him that it was quite out of the question that he should wait for me and that I had only just arrived. 'So much the better,' he said. 'And now, let me welcome you in my own house and tell you how glad I am to see you here.'

He took me to the window to show me the view. 'Look at this scenery,' he said. 'I like it; it's so restful, the best possible *milieu* for my work: these vast peaceful fields going right down to the lake.'

42

The door to the dining-room opened and I was introduced to Madame Sibelius and her second daughter, whereupon I was asked to sit down to table. The dining-room was built in the old Northern style. Opposite the entrance there was a large open chimney-piece, and the walls consisted of solid round logs painted brown.

The altogether charming conversation was agreeably stimulated by a bottle of good claret, and the salad definitely proved to have been prepared by the hand of a master. It is impossible to imagine a more perfect host than Sibelius. He combines with the great kindliness and exquisite manners of a *grand seigneur* the fascinating talk and wide outlook of a great intellectual.

I told Sibelius that I liked to see the universal spirit in him, as musicians unfortunately tend to be self-centred and lacking in general perception. 'It is perhaps because I have always been so fond of the classics that I am interested in all those things,' he said. And he added: 'You know, Horace was the great love of my youth.' Once when I met Sibelius in Rome I offered him a glass of good golden Frascati, asking him what he thought of it. 'It is wonderful,' he said. 'So full of poetry. It reminds me of the Odes of Horace.'

At luncheon that day he also spoke of the Greeks.

'Of course I had the greatest admiration for them as a child,' he said. 'But you know, we read much less Greek than Latin at school, and this rather damped my ardour. I followed the events of the Iliad with passionate interest. But, having read that one hero challenged another, it was such a nuisance waiting till next lesson and sometimes even until next week to learn who was victor in the duel and who was killed. We boys used to fight each other every day, so you can imagine what a strain that meant to my youthful temperament.'

One of Sibelius' chief interests is historical reading. At table he discussed different historical and political matters. There was something original, picturesque and amusing about his view of every subject he mentioned. I could not help expressing my surprise at finding him so well informed about things entirely outside the world of music. 'You know,' he said, smiling, 'I once had rather an amusing experience when travelling in Sweden.' It so happened that he had recently read an important historical work on a subject which particularly interested him. Opposite him in the railway compartment was a man, and they began to talk. After a while Sibelius discovered that his travelling-companion was a well-known Swedish historian. He therefore turned the conversation to the book which

44

he had been reading. There followed a long discussion, which gave Sibelius an opportunity of setting out his views on the subject, to which his fellow traveller appeared to listen with much interest. At the end of the journey Sibelius produced his card. His interlocutor, under the impression that he had been spending the day with a colleague, now discovered, much to his surprise, that he had been enjoying the company of the greatest composer of the Northern countries, though not a word had been said about music during the whole day.

This anecdote may be considered symbolical of Sibelius' conversation on many occasions. That day, for instance, no musical subject was mentioned at luncheon.

After luncheon Sibelius and I shut ourselves up in the drawing-room and I showed him my humble attempt at orchestrating the first movement of Beethoven's great C-major sonata. Of course it was all wrong, except perhaps for some very brief passages. It is characteristic of Sibelius that he at once pointed out the few positive points and discussed them extensively. 'You know, it is much easier to criticize than to admire,' he declared. But being very conscientious he went through the whole score. There was no negative criticism; on the contrary, in every single case he explained how to change the score and improve it. In many cases he suggested more than one solution to a difficulty. Having been through the whole score, he formulated some general remarks.

'Your respect for Beethoven has been too great. Remember, this sonata is a work for the piano, whereas I asked you to write an orchestral score. The public must never feel that your instrumentation is a translation from some other idiom; they must understand that it is the original text.' And he added: 'You have no idea how often I feel the translation when I listen to the first performance of a new orchestral work in a concert-hall.'

From this he went on to discuss some of the classical composers, and he declared Beethoven to be the master whom he had always admired above all others as the great dominating figure in the art of music. 'I have been brought up with the idea', he proceeded, 'that Beethoven's string quartettes are to be venerated as the Bible, being a sacred text, in which no human being would dare to change anything. Do you know, I have had in my life an indirect impression of his personality. In my young days I studied in Vienna, and my piano was once tuned by an old man who used to tune Beethoven's piano during his last years.' Sibelius suddenly grew silent and remained so for a while. Then, as if continuing the thoughts that had absorbed him, he said slowly and in a low voice: 'And it was wonderful to look into those eyes, which had seen the master of the Ninth symphony.'

He again paused for a moment, then came back to the subject of instrumentation. 'Do you know', he asked, 'whom I consider the two greatest geniuses of the orchestra? You will be surprised to hear it: Mozart and Mendelssohn.'

Sibelius said this about six months after the completion of the first version of his Fifth symphony, a version which unfortunately has never been printed. Certainly he must always have professed a great admiration for the orchestral workmanship of the master of the *Magic Flute* and the musical poet who wrote the score to the *Midsummer Night's Dream*; but in his youth and early manhood he would have pronounced his judgment less categorically. The period at which he uttered the words quoted above preceded the conception of his Sixth symphony. After the voluntary exile of the Fourth symphony he had come back to life to praise all its beauty in his next great work, which ends in a triumphant hymn. Then a new phase opened in the mental evolution of the master. Once more he abandoned the glories of surrounding life to look inward, but this time he did so with a serenity of mind,

47

which he had never before experienced. Like Goethe he must have said in his heart:

Und mich ergreift ein längst entwöhntes Sehnen,
Nach jenem stillen, ernsten Geisterreich.

So the ground was prepared for the Sixth symphony, that ascetic, crystalline ode, so curiously akin to the later works of Palestrina. But a new style had to be created, for only a transformed and transcendent orchestral language would express the atmosphere of this maiden world, so far beyond the ephemeral passions and joys of daily life. The palette could comprise only the most sober colours. But the restrictions of medium, which Sibelius thus imposed on himself, involved an overwhelming increase of all the artistic and technical difficulties. The composer had to appeal to all his long experience and his genius to create an idiom with the required qualities: the richness and variety within the narrow limits, the serenity, clearness, transparency. These are, of course, the outstanding qualities of Mozart's and Mendelssohn's orchestration; and Sibelius' saying, quoted above, gives the key to a right understanding of the score of his own Sixth symphony.

After he had expressed his great admiration for the subtle orchestral language of the two German masters, Sibelius told me: 'To my mind a Mozart allegro is the most perfect model for a symphonic movement. Think of its wonderful unity and homogeneity! It is like an uninterrupted flowing, where nothing stands out and nothing encroaches upon the rest.'

In these words, as in his remarks at the rehearsal of his own Fourth symphony, Sibelius expressed his general artistic conviction. It was the epic poet and symphonist once more insisting on the importance of unity in a work of art and its parts.

But Sibelius' admiration for Mozart and the classical school goes beyond this. An analysis of the form of his work will show it to be a direct continuation of the symphonic architecture elaborated in Central Europe in the second part of the eighteenth century.

Everybody knows that the symphony, the string quartette and the sonata all represent the same form of musical architecture. Most of my readers will also have learnt that the name sonata is used equally to label a particular kind of movement as distinct, for instance, from the rondo. The sonata in this sense of the word consists of three parts. In the first part all the elements are set out. It opens on the main subject (Hauptsatz), which is followed by a transition (Übergangssatz). Sometimes this transition brings out a new element, sometimes it only continues the main subject. It leads over to the second subject (Seitensatz) which forms a contrast to the preceding elements and is in a different key. The first part of the sonata finishes on the conclusion (Schluss-satz), very often followed by a coda, which every now and then echoes the main subject. In the second part, the 'working out', the preceding elements are developed, varied, combined and set out in different keys. The third part is built up like the first, except that the second subject invariably appears on the same tonic as that of the main subject. The transition is sometimes omitted from this part of the sonata if in the beginning it was only based on the main subject. After the third part a huge coda can be added to the sonata, a sort of second 'working out'. This big coda, not to be confused with the small coda following the conclusion, forms an outstanding feature of some of Beethoven's most famous works—for instance, the first movement of the Kreutzer sonata.

The classical masters use the architecture of the sonata almost exclusively for quick movements. In their symphonies, string quartettes, trios and sonatas the first movement is practically always built up on the scheme of the sonata-form, the other movements being rondos, etc. Two famous exceptions may be quoted. In Beethoven's C-sharp minor sonata the first movement is a prelude and the finale a sonata. And the first of the master's three Rasoumowsky quartettes contains two sonatas, the first movement and the adagio.

The first movements of Sibelius' first two symphonies are built up like the corresponding parts of Mozart's symphonic works. In the long series of Sibelius' compositions it is the first two symphonies which evoke the magic spell of the North with a particular power and intensity. Their monumental style and heroic romanticism, adding new and unknown words to the idiom of the preceding masters, are unique in the history of music. It would seem that these two works could have nothing in common with the rules of italianizing Mozartean classicism and its eighteenth-century grace. The first movement of the Second symphony, especially, might be taken to refute any such connection. Kajanus, speaking of the Second symphony, once remarked that Sibelius in this work expressed himself by *aphorisms*; and no better description is possible. The main subject of the first movement contains several aphorisms launched one after another. They may strike us as rather fortuitous, as having no function in a symphonic movement; moreover they are even likely to bewilder us by their form, structure and orchestration. But a further study of the score will show that

51

everything has been most carefully thought out. The movement being a sonata, the main subject returns after the 'working out'. And now the bizarre aphorisms fit beautifully into the whole, forming an expressive accompaniment to the opening theme. There is no big coda at the end of the movement, such as we often find in Beethoven's work. Thus this first part of Sibelius' Second symphony, in spite of all differences, preserves the form of a Mozart allegro.

We have already seen that the classical composers nearly always reserved the architecture of the sonata for the first movement of their symphonies, string quartettes, trios and sonatas. If we are surprised to find Sibelius adopting this form in the first part of his first two symphonies, still, in doing so, he only made his own new and revolutionary inspirations conform to the canon of the expiring rococo. But the score of the Second symphony has another and even more surprising feature. An analysis of the famous finale of this work, one of the master's greatest conceptions, will show that this, too, has been built up like a classical sonata-movement. Thus it is the second of its kind in the same score, which is exceptional even in classical works. And having no big coda like those to be found in Beethoven's work, this essentially original finale again preserves the form

of a Mozart allegro. (11) Like all true innovators—
and unlike those whose bloodless, intellectual pro-
ductions aim at overthrowing the great traditions in
art—Sibelius believes that the new and transform-
ing ideas must come from within, not from the
exterior form. And like Dante he is a revolutionary
by temperament although a conservative by opinion.

Sibelius' saying about the Mozart allegros is therefore no mere phrase. Here again practice supports
theory. True, the Mozartean form is not preserved
intact in Sibelius' later works. The outlines and the
architectural design are gradually transformed, and
eventually the master arrives at entirely new conceptions. Yet all this subsequent evolution has its
origin in the clear and transparent form of the
sonata-movements in the first two symphonies—
just as Velazquez' third manner is based upon the
two preceding phases of his work.

Perhaps somebody will remark that Sibelius' particular appreciation of Mozart's orchestration does
not fit in with the admiration he professes for
Beethoven, whom, as we saw, he regards as the
master above all others. As a matter of fact there is
no contradiction whatever, as another saying of his
will show.

One day he told me: 'Orchestration is the discom-
fiture of absolute idealism.' As I looked rather

puzzled, he continued: 'Suppose you want to write a cantabile for the violoncello, and your theme requires the colour of the A string—what will you do if the melodic line carries you below the A? Either you will have to accept the D string which is just as hypocritical as on the violin—or else transpose the whole theme. In both cases your absolute idealism is being defeated by the material difficulties of life. And if you want an heroic theme to be given by the trumpets and it happens to soar too high, you must either renounce the colour of the trumpets or have it transposed. Orchestration is like life, a hard struggle for existence. All the more precious the victory and the capacity of saving your ideas in spite of all obstacles.

'But there is another side to the question too, and here again you will have to reckon with practical difficulties. Even when you see no immediate obstacles to the exteriorization of your ideas, you must not forget to reckon with all the little imperfections of which there are so many in the orchestra. It is always important to keep in touch with the realities of life. I, for instance, am glad of every material contact with the orchestra, and I call all the concerts conducted by me *orchestral baths*. Believe me, they are very important for your musical health, because without them you might grow too idealistic.'

This idea of Sibelius affords the possibility of understanding his view on Mozart's orchestration and that of Beethoven. The master of the Nine symphonies was far too strong and severe a personality to comply with anything that would encroach upon the sovereignty of his ideas. On the other hand, the imperfections of the orchestra were far more numerous in his day than in ours. When Beethoven achieves marvellous instrumental effects he owes it more to the overwhelming power of his genius and inspiration than to a particular sense of orchestration. With Mozart it is quite different. His childlike lovable mind found no difficulty in accepting the restrictions imposed by the orchestra of the rococo. He was therefore more a man of the orchestra than Beethoven.

Many composers have felt the hardship of the struggle with the realities of the orchestra. Sibelius' own work is full of striking and instructive examples. Often the free development of his inspiration seems to have been hampered by the lack of dynamic intensity in the lower register of the trombones. In his Fourth and Seventh symphonies, for instance, there are crescendi and fortissimi, which cannot be brought out properly. (12) At other times you feel that he has had difficulty with the bassoons. And the result is that he requires them to play, pianissimo, a chromatic passage in the lower register, where neither modulations nor pianissimi are possible. (13) A further development of instrumental mechanism will probably make a satisfactory rendering of these passages quite easy. In his masterly extended edition of Berlioz' treatise on orchestration, Richard Strauss expresses the opinion that a composer by requiring what is actually impossible very often stimulates makers of instruments to further progress and perfection. The bold writing of some passages in Sibelius' scores may therefore be regarded as prophetic of the unknown possibilities of the future.

V

When next I visited Sibelius, he seemed really pleased with the work I had done. I mention this because it shows his extraordinary kindness and the touching personal interest he took in his pupil. He told me that there was a notable progress in what I showed him this time, and then followed no end of congratulations. Eventually he declared that he felt highly satisfied, seeing that he had been of some use. He thereupon looked at me as if something particularly pleasant had occurred and once more added: 'I am only too glad if I can be of some help to you.' His words contained no touch of exaggeration. In spite of the unique triumphs he has scored, he has retained the freshness and candour of his mind, unlike so many other artists, who have been completely ruined by successes of minor importance. You feel the greatness of the man no less in such small episodes than when hearing him expound his ideas.

Sibelius then turned to my modest attempt and said: 'Up to the present your scores have looked too much like the piano style of Schubert. It is the usual fault with the first efforts of young composers. But now it is different; there are open spaces in this score: you feel the fresh air coming in through the window. This time you have brought life into it and opened free vistas on either side.'

His comparison between the piano style of Schubert and the first attempts of young composers by no means implies disparagement of the great romantic master. On the contrary Sibelius speaks with the greatest enthusiasm of the ever flowing inspiration and eternal youth of Schubert's innumerable songs, his great string quartettes and the Unfinished symphony.

As usual, this lesson presently turned into a general discussion. 'What do you think of Wagner?' Sibelius suddenly asked me. I told him that I had the greatest admiration for his genius, but that there were certain things in his personality, and consequently in his music, which I did not like. 'Yes, exactly,' he chimed in. 'Wagner is rude, brutal, vulgar and completely lacking in delicacy! For instance, he shouts: "I love you, I love you." ' Sibelius suddenly stopped; then after a moment he said in quite a different tone: 'To my mind it is something that you should whisper.'

There exists a work of Sibelius which gives the finest possible musical illustration of this idea, the little suite for string orchestra called *Rakastava*, the lover. An ethereal atmosphere is here evoked with an unusual magic. The writing for muted strings is of a loveliness exceptional even in the work of Sibelius. Their subtle murmur seems to bring us a message from a distant world; only the pianissimo of violins and violas may whisper these thoughts in our ears—nobody would dare to express them quite openly. It is a pity that this infinitely delicate work is but little known, and it is to be hoped that it will no longer remain so. As a matter of fact, it is sure to find admirers everywhere, except perhaps among the more ferocious intellectuals.

Sibelius' violent reaction to the Wagnerian method of shouting 'I love you' is also a deliberate protest against a whole attitude towards life.

Moreover Sibelius as a musician and composer is decidedly opposed to the creator of the German musical drama. He told me how strongly he objected to the heaviness and rhetorical exaggeration of Wagner's musical style. Indeed, there is in the art of music nothing more alien to the mind of Sibelius than the overloaded baroque of Wagner. As we have seen, Sibelius never abandoned his own convictions for the experiments of the modernistic school; to his mind these deviations were episodes merely, and he was never greatly disturbed by them. He even grants them a certain moral and historical value, since in some cases they may have helped to abolish old-fashioned conventionalism. With Wagner it is different. Sibelius' personal dislike of him is further increased by the conviction that the influence of that master and his whole school has been disastrous to the evolution of music.

Sibelius concluded his remarks on Wagner by saying: 'Look at his orchestration, that mass of different instruments in unison! Wagner reminds me of his former friend and later antagonist Nietzsche, who always suggests a butler who has been created a baron.'

Sibelius now spoke of the situation in the musical world of his youth. 'At the time when I produced my first orchestral works,' he said, 'Wagner was the last word. Every composer thought it his moral duty to fill twenty or thirty lines all the way through in his scores and I was looked upon as a very strange creature because I did not do so.'

These reminiscences led Sibelius to touch upon one of his favourite subjects. He insisted on the importance of writing frankly what one feels, instead of subscribing to the passing vogue of the day. 'I know it takes a good deal of courage to do that,' he said, and then quoted some quite forgotten composers like Bungert, who had been considered great geniuses in their lifetime. As a contrast to them he mentioned Brahms, who has outlived them all, although he refused out of pure conservatism to believe in any further evolution of musical language. The way Sibelius opposed Bungert to Brahms was highly characteristic. 'Bungert was proclaimed a second Wagner,' he began, and then told me how every possible chance in life seemed to have been offered to Bungert by the benevolent goddesses of fate. With Brahms it was quite the contrary. The gigantic shadow of Wagner at first seemed to leave him no chance of a place in the sun. Sibelius had excellent opportunity, when studying in Vienna, to watch the rivalry between the Wagnerian current and the partisans of Brahms. He even took part in the struggle indirectly by joining an 'anti-Wagnerian' orchestra, founded by some young and enterprising enthusiasts. 'And now nobody remembers Bungert,' he said. 'You, for instance, had not even heard his name when I mentioned it. From that you can see how no advantages, however great, can save a composer if he has no intrinsic value.' He added that he considered the ever-increasing glory of Brahms, compared to the complete oblivion of 'the second Wagner,' of far-reaching moral significance.

Sibelius now turned his attention to the orchestration of Brahms, the heavy pianistic and primitive character of which is well known to all concertgoers. He concluded by saying: 'Everything written by a genius is interesting, whatever his aesthetic ideas may be, and in spite of all his mistakes and imperfections.' Suddenly he added: 'Did you know that I met Brahms in Vienna? He always offered people cigars, but before meeting him I was told that one was not supposed to accept them.'

The atmosphere of Vienna seems to have made a profound and lasting impression on the mind of Sibelius, for he speaks of it often and enthusiastically. No doubt a considerable part of his vast output, although perhaps not his highest inspirations, originates in memories of his stay as a young man in the Austrian capital. He has, for instance, retained a marked predilection for waltzes. Everybody knows the numerous compositions in this kind which have issued from his pen. The most important of them is the famous *Valse Triste*. It is a pity that it has become too popular. Most people, hearing it played by restaurant orchestras, instead of in its original symphonic setting, do not realize that it is a piece of music of great originality and fine workmanship.

There is nothing surprising in the fact that Sibelius, the great symphonist, takes such obvious delight in waltzes. This is not a weakness, as some of the master's antagonists have tried to insinuate. Everybody knows Brahms' great love of waltzes, but nobody ever thought that the grandeur and dignity of his symphonic conception were impaired by it. And Tchaikowsky goes further still: the score of his Fifth symphony contains a waltz in place of a scherzo. Yet to my knowledge this fact has never been used as a serious argument against the great Russian master.

But there is another section of Sibelius' compositions, more or less akin to the waltzes, which seems to have perplexed even sincere admirers of his genius: I mean all the light piano pieces, etc., of which there is such a profusion in his work. No doubt they are largely reminiscent of the enchanting city on the Danube. I have already quoted Sibelius saying half in jest that he is wont to write piano pieces in his free moments. In spite of the deliberately exaggerated humorous touch, these words yet give us the key to a right understanding of all this part of Sibelius' work. His numerous light compositions mean to the master a relaxation, a rest from the heavier creative tasks incumbent on him.

Thus they only form a modern counterpart to a feature well known in the history of music. Between his great operas Gluck, for instance, used to write ballets for the court of Vienna, and the work of Mozart is interspersed with serenatas and other compositions written for various occasions. To both masters these minor pieces meant a rest from the great emanations of their genius, and similarly Sibelius spends his 'free moments' between the creation of his more important symphonic works writing lighter piano pieces.

Having spoken of the atmosphere of Vienna, Sibelius was naturally led to compare it to that of the French capital. 'I think Paris is an excellent place for working,' he said. 'It stimulates one's energy. I know it from my own experience.' He told me how strongly he had felt this in Paris and in Saint-Germain, overlooking the city, where he had once spent several months, working at one of his symphonies. 'It is a pity', he added, 'that fifth-rate composers seem to score such great successes in Paris.'

And now he enlarged upon this subject, which is for him of vital importance: the essential difference between what is only the passing fashion of the moment, and style in the genuine work of art, which will appeal to generation after generation. He told me that he thought Paris particularly incited artists to search for new means of expression and that he made no doubt this influence would prove most useful for the further development of art, if understood in the right way. Only the public should not be confronted with mere experiments, which unfortunately seemed to invade the concert-halls more and more. Every search for new harmonic tissue, every pursuit of unknown orchestral colour, be it systematic or improvised and spontaneous, should remain subordinate to the creative imagination of the artist. Only thus would the composer preserve his spiritual independence, his individuality; only thus would his conceptions assume the character of a work of art, being the true expression of ideas suggested to the author by his inspiration, supported by solid technical knowledge and experience.

It is interesting to see these ideas reflected in Sibelius' own work. His first two symphonies are especially apt for our context. When they were first brought before the public they were justly considered revolutionary; but within thirty years their exceptional popularity has conferred upon them a halo: they are already classics. What impresses us in these two powerful works is not the material innovation of the symphonic structure, but the intense originality and significance of the musical images on which they are built up. A rich series of ideas, embracing every shade from the proudest heroism to the subtlest lyric sentiment, dominates these two scores. In writing them Sibelius certainly did not think of creating something *new*; he simply listened to his irresistible, volcanic inspiration and accepted its direction. The personal colour of the orchestral language is not intellectually thought out, but spontaneously created and entirely conditioned by the individual character and atmosphere of the music. A closer study of the scores will corroborate this.

The harmonic tissue is of an almost embarrassing simplicity. The master has evidently given it this rather archaic character so that it shall remain a discreet background, and not distract the listener's attention from the themes. A similar economy will be found in subsequent scores. Even in Sibelius' later works, whose harmonization is at times extremely complex, there are passages consisting of plain common chords, where these happen to suit the master's purpose. The structure of each episode is imposed on it by its intrinsic character and not by a desire to experiment. It is refreshing to see such courage and independence of mind in an age which considers a certain amount of fortuitous discordant notes quite as necessary in any serious score as is a dazzling hussar's uniform to a tamer of lions.

The problem of counterpoint is faced by Sibelius in his first two symphonies in a way which accords with his treatment of the harmonic tissue. The polyphonic, imitative episode in the scherzo of the First symphony illustrates his principles at this period. It suddenly changes to plain homophonous writing at the moment when further elaboration would spoil the freshness of the musical image. In this respect the imitative passages in the last movement of the same symphony are similar. The finale of the Second symphony, being a sonata, contains a 'working out'. If we compare this 'working out' to the corresponding part of the first movement of the First symphony, we find some interesting and instructive analogies. In both cases the polyphonic elaboration of the themes is reduced to essentials, being entirely subordinate to the entity of the musical image instead of dominating it. In Sibelius' later works a considerable evolution of the counterpoint can be discerned; the renaissance style of the Sixth symphony is a very good instance. Yet the master's attitude has undergone no change since the time when he wrote his first two symphonies. Here too the conception of the musical image entirely dominates the whole score, and the elaboration of structure is still subordinate. The increase of the polyphonic element is a necessary consequence of the intrinsic character of the themes; it only emphasizes their individuality instead of encroaching on it. From this we may infer that Sibelius' attitude to counterpoint is consistent with the idea so plainly expressed in his purely homophonous writing. Neither of these complementary modes of expression has ever been allowed to become a field of experiment in his work.

It is a characteristic of Sibelius' orchestration that he apparently uses individual instruments, small groups of instruments and the ensemble at their simplest. Nothing could be more strongly opposed to the spirit of experiment. Though he appreciates the value of deliberate researches for new means of expression, if understood in the right way, Sibelius has never gone in for anything of the kind in his own work, either in harmonic conception, polyphonic tissue or orchestral colour.

After he had spoken of the atmosphere of Paris, Sibelius turned the conversation to the founder of the new French school of music. 'Debussy has caught the spirit of Paris,' he said, and asked me what I thought of the French composer. I told him that I often considered Debussy a worker of quite exquisite *bibelots*. But to my mind, I added, he was completely lacking in grandeur and depth although undoubtedly a genius. 'I quite understand what you mean,' Sibelius answered. 'Still the music of Debussy was a word at the right moment, in my opinion.' And he added that there are artists, whose importance for the further development of art is greater than the intrinsic value of their work. 'Besides,' he said, 'Debussy himself knew very well that he was neither grand nor profound. I know, because I have met him.' Sibelius then told me that many years ago in London he shared a concert with Debussy. Each in turn conducted his own work and during the interval they had an opportunity of talking to one another. It was during this conversation that Debussy made Sibelius understand that he realized the limits of his own importance. This statement is particularly interesting because it is just the opposite of what we are usually told about the personality of the French composer. Enthusiasts, writing of Debussy, have tried to proclaim him the sovereign creator of all the music of the future; and many anecdotes would seem to indicate that he was by no means lacking in self-reliance. Indeed, he could justly feel proud of having enriched the art of music by creating a new idiom of infinite subtlety, a language of most delicate tints and shades. But confronted by Sibelius, his usual self-confidence may have shrunk. The volcanic temperament of the great Northern symphonist perhaps made him realize temporarily what nature had refused him.

Sibelius finished the unusually long discussion of this day by emphasizing the importance of going abroad every now and then—leaving the well-known surroundings of one's daily life to gain fresh and stimulating impressions. This idea is highly characteristic of the Northern mentality. It brings to mind Ibsen, writing *A Doll's House* during a winter at Amalfi, or finding the definite formula for *Brand* one warm day when entering St. Peter's in Rome. Many other examples could be quoted from the history of Northern art and literature.

But Sibelius' last words were: 'Although I like seeing other countries and staying in foreign cities for a time, I must *live* in Finland. I could never abandon this country for good; that would finish me, and mean death to my art!'

VI

The monumental series of Sibelius' symphonies is a unique structure in contemporary music. But it also forms the nucleus of the master's own vast output, all his other works being grouped round this gigantic central column. Sibelius' personal conception of the symphony as a manifestation of art and the spirit of man may therefore be considered fundamental for his aesthetic philosophy and his opinions on life. Before we attempt to isolate this conception, some generalizations must be made.

Some ten years ago one of the leading composers of the new school solemnly declared in an interview that Beethoven's work was of minor importance— real music originated in his own scores. And he communicated to us another notion of considerable interest: the symphony being dead, it would be utterly ridiculous to attempt to revive it.

This assertion is based on an idea which has been admitted without discussion by many protagonists of innovation in art, the idea that the biological and mental qualifications of our artistic perception might suddenly be subject to a complete transformation.

Yet the heart of man has not changed in two thousand years, his sorrows and joys, disillusions and exultations have remained the same for twenty centuries. It is hardly possible to realize what a vast space of time separates, let us say, Lucretius and Alfred de Musset—some episodes of *De Rerum Natura* seem to be contemporary to the introduction of *Rolla*. There are pages in the work of Renaissance philosophers like Pomponazzi and Montaigne which express the sociological ideas of the last twenty years, and some of St. Benedict's advice in his monastic rule offers examples of the most subtle modern psychology. Since the mind and heart of mankind have remained the same for so long, it would be more courageous than reasonable to credit their sudden transformation within the course of a few years. This being the case, it is also hard to see why the intrinsic foundation of our perception of art should change, although its exterior manifestations present the greatest variety according to the different characters of subsequent epochs.

Since the time of Heraclitus and Parmenides, the

dawn of Greek philosophy, Western thought seems to have divided into two essential currents: 'Everything flows,' the famous saying of Heraclitus, in opposition to Parmenides' insistence on unity everywhere. Parmenides, and all the later philosophers of the school of Elea, express the *epic* attitude towards life. Through classical Antiquity, the Middle Ages, the Renaissance period and modern times, the contrast between the ideas of Parmenides and of Heraclitus makes itself more or less strongly felt. It expresses the incompatibility of two different kinds of temperament, which no doubt will be there as long as mankind exists. And since the epic temperament will be represented in the further development of philosophy it will also be represented in the art of the future. Musically speaking, this means that the symphonic line will always find adepts, although very few—as in the past—will be found strong enough for the heavy task incumbent on them.

Symphonies belonging to the current repertoire divide into three essentially different types. The symphonic masterpieces of Haydn and Mozart are the classical representatives of the first type. Here we find the epic idea at its simplest. It dominates the whole work, conferring upon it an unsurpassed serenity, transparency and homogeneity.

The immortal creations of the late eighteenth century find their more modern counterpart in the symphonies of Brahms and Bruckner. Nothing could be more epic than these scores, overwhelming emanations as they are of two profoundly philosophical geniuses, ultimately unable to express themselves in the language of the orchestra, and yet obliged to speak this language. In spite of the far more elaborate harmonic tissue and the great richness in themes and lyrical episodes—chiefly in Bruckner—both masters still preserve the calm, simple outlook of their spiritual ancestors of the eighteenth century. It is no coincidence that the last movement of Brahms' last symphony is a chaconne, that is to say variations over a bass-part, one of the most epic forms of musical architecture. And Bruckner, the last man to write an adagio after Beethoven, inserts many of his purest religious inspirations in the scores of his symphonies, thus investing them with the classical epic architecture instead of giving us lyrical hymns.

To understand the grandeur of the epic line as represented by Haydn, Mozart, Brahms and Bruckner it suffices to quote Gustaf Mahler, one of the most pathetic cases in the history of music. Nothing is intellectually more interesting than the scores of his symphonies. He certainly aims at vast epic perspectives, and his intentions are supported by un-failing technical skill and experience. Yet all these undoubtedly great qualities avail him nothing, for there is no life in these gigantic works, conceived as they are without inspiration, *invito Apolline*. They are, indeed, of no importance for the further development of the symphonic form.

The second type of symphony is diametrically opposed to Mahler's work. The scores of the Viennese composer, although characteristic specimens of true symphonic music, will sink into oblivion because they lack intrinsic life. But the works of which I am now speaking are sure to fascinate future generations. They are symphonic in spirit, if not in form. Such is the beauty and power of the themes and musical images on which they are built up, and so fine is even their architectural construction on occasion, that these qualities outweigh any discrepancies.

This second type is represented by the so-called symphonies of Schubert, Berlioz and Tchaikowsky.

The Unfinished symphony of the young Viennese composer is nearly an epic work, so surprisingly homogeneous is the inherent spirit and the exterior character of this amazing score. Yet Schubert here —as always—proceeds by episodes, however brilliantly linked, and it is the dazzling individual beauty of all these images and not their unity that gives the work eternal youth.

Berlioz' two famous works, *Symphonie Fantastique* and *Harold en Italie*, are much farther from being symphonic. The exalted romanticism and sensibility of the composer as well as the obviously dramatic and lyric character of these two scores are strongly opposed to the unity of the broad, epic outlook. Moreover, magical though these qualities are in intensifying the different episodes, on the other hand they sometimes spoil the architecture of the whole. Yet, in a century, however full of important musical events, no tarnish has appeared on the fresh colours of these two scores.

The case of Tchaikowsky is rather similar to that of the great French composer, although, except for the orchestra, where Berlioz will always remain unsurpassed, the workmanship of Tchaikowsky is far superior to the somewhat deficient structure and heterogeneous architectural design of the two French symphonies. Tchaikowsky's harmonic tissue is perhaps not always original; but it is invariably homogeneous. Moreover, in every single case it most beautifully suits the purpose of the author and at moments attains a profoundly expressive character. When Tchaikowsky resorts to counterpoint he never spoils the unity of the otherwise plainly homophonous structure; he uses the polyphonic element only as a means of adding new accents to his language. The great unity of style is still further enhanced by the perfectly logical architectural design. Nothing could be more homogeneous than Tchaikowsky's symphonies, or rather the last three of them. These masterpieces rank among the finest examples of symphonic architecture—and yet they are not epically conceived, their spirit is not symphonic; for Tchaikowsky is too much the Slav, and happily he never tried to be anything else, in spite of the 'italianizing' element in his work, which is of no importance, though his antagonists have made much of it. He never achieves the broad epic outlook, being too intensely fascinated by the charm of each single episode, the spell of its thematic beauty and the suggestive power of its orchestral colouring.

Between the essentially epic form of Haydn, Mozart, Brahms and Bruckner on one side, and its more picturesque derivations as represented by Schubert, Berlioz and Tchaikowsky on the other, a third type of symphony has been created, the noblest, the most overpowering of all. It embraces the epic outlook, the profound perspectives of the first type as well as the intensity of temperament and fantasy of the second—qualities which logically should exclude each other. Only Beethoven could imagine such a scheme, only the greatest of all masters could carry it out. Within the large scope of this personal conception of the symphony he realized another miracle, perhaps even more astonishing than the idea itself. Though he had to go beyond the elegance and charm of the expiring rococo, and pass through a period of great dramatic conflict, to reach the serenity of contemplation, no slackening whatever can be noticed in the volcanic intensity of his temperament, from his earliest works to his last.

This long digression has been necessary in order to assign to Sibelius his place in the evolution of the symphonic idea. I have described Beethoven as the 'third type', but it must be understood that representatives of the 'second type' like, for instance, Tchaikowsky, partly derive from him.

Sibelius is an adherent of the third type. I have already quoted him saying that he considers Beethoven the master 'above all others'. True, this means nothing by itself; in spite of the highbrow fashion for disparaging the master of the Nine symphonies, hundreds of composers will still be found professing the most sincere admiration for him, without being able to follow his lead. But in this case the admiration is more significant, and Sibelius' words assume great importance if other sayings of his are taken into account.

Sibelius' style in his earlier period has often been compared to Tchaikowsky's. The first two symphonies of the Finnish master have thus been considered characteristic of the second type of symphonic writing, and even now they are sometimes performed accordingly. This is a great mistake. A careful and unprejudiced study of the scores will show that they continue the line of Beethoven. Yet the affinity to the atmosphere evoked by Tchaikowsky is unmistakable. Evidently the roots of the problem lie farther below the surface than one might at first suppose.

The temperament of Tchaikowsky oscillates between exaltation, violent outbursts of passion, and submission without the slightest resistance. If we consider the mental climate of Sibelius as it is expressed in his first two symphonies, we certainly find some affinity to that of Tchaikowsky; and at the same time we find differences which are far more important. There is no *exaltation* in Sibelius' scores, the feeling of triumph and joy expressed by him being less occasional, much more virile, heroic and organically connected with the rest of the work. In Sibelius' first symphonies the impressive flames of a fire which is constantly burning form the counterpart to the violent outbursts of Tchaikowsky. On the other hand, there is nothing in Sibelius' work that

79

corresponds to the submission which is so characteristic of Tchaikowsky. Even his most subtle lyrical episodes are entirely without this tendency, so typically Slav and oriental. The contrast is fundamental.

One day when Sibelius told me of his admiration for the genius of Tchaikowsky, he concluded by saying that the Russian master gives himself up to every situation without looking beyond the moment. These words contain the solution of a problem which seems to have embarrassed many critics and concert-goers; they clearly define the difference between Sibelius' mentality and Tchaikowsky's. 'Looking beyond the moment' is the essence of the epic, the broad symphonic outlook; it means *thinking in perspective*. Simple though this may appear, we must consider the matter more fully.

I shall take as my starting-point an idea which has been beautifully developed by Plato, and I may take some liberties with it. Suppose we are walking up a hill and stop in front of a wide view, we may see in the far distance some huge mountains which will to our visual perception seem quite small compared to the tiny little bushes in the foreground. But reflection will tell us at once that these mountains are in fact far bigger than all the objects in our surroundings. This is where the epic element, thinking in perspective, comes in. The same phenomenon can

80

be noticed within the range of thought, though naturally in a less obvious form.

A child seeing some sweetmeats will probably be tempted to eat them although he knows that he is not supposed to do so. If in spite of the prohibition he still takes them, this means that he has been induced to do so by the immediate visual perception. The sweetmeats being in the foreground of his mental vision, they assume far larger proportions than repentance and punishment coming farther behind. If on the contrary the child resists the temptation, he gives an example of thinking in perspective at its simplest. He then realizes that the pleasure of eating bonbons is very small compared to the discomfort of punishment and repentance. This is in fact far more important than the satisfaction of a moment's whim, although at first sight it seemed much smaller, being in the background. Montaigne said that there would be no drunkards if the illness came first and the stimulating effects of wine afterwards.

The great epic writers, like Goethe and Gottfried Keller, never lose sight of the whole. At every moment they measure the more ephemeral importance of all the episodes in life, whatever their fascination, sorrow or joy, by the comprehensive outlines of our existence. This is made possible by their faculty of thinking in perspective. Lyric poets face life in the opposite way. The spell of romance, the exultation of success and the dejection of adversity completely absorb them, to the exclusion of any mental measuring capacity. Episodes in the foreground of their minds assume such colour as to falsify the tones of the background.

It is only natural that music should provide analogies to the evidence of literature. Tchaikowsky for instance represents the extreme of that temperament, whose intensity excludes any measuring capacity, and his art culminates in his last symphony, that apotheosis of dejection and submission. Nothing could be more alien to the mind of Sibelius, even in his early period, than the spirit which dominates the *Symphonie Pathétique*. For although endowed by nature with a temperament of truly volcanic intensity he is never absorbed by any situation or episode to the detriment of the whole. Thus he declares himself an adept of the line initiated by Beethoven, who of all composers is the most typical symphonist, though the ardour of his temperament would seem to exclude any possibility of epic perspectives. I have already mentioned the aphorisms in the first part of Sibelius' Second symphony. At first they seem to have been inserted in the score as independent episodes placed one after another; towards the end of the movement, however, they are seen to form a most expressive accompaniment to the first theme. This is highly characteristic of the true epic conception. Every aphorism has an individuality of its own; yet in the composer's mind each is only considered as one of the innumerable carved stones to be used for the construction of the large building. Sibelius' work is scattered with examples of the same kind.

The exquisite Third symphony has remained in undeserved obscurity. It leads to the Fourth, that very interesting and unprecedented case in the history of music. Every concert-goer will have felt in it a very complicated mental conflict with the most far-reaching consequences for the author himself. This impression is corroborated when Sibelius speaks of the work. Not that he would give me the slightest hint as to the exact meaning of it. He only gave me to understand how much this score meant to him personally.

After the isolation of the Fourth symphony, a return to life is expressed in the Fifth. There are parts of this score which are nearer to Beethoven in spirit than any other work of Sibelius. We find once again an intimate contact with the world of men. Yet there is a change. The master's general attitude remains epic, as in the beginning, but his manner of facing life's problems has undergone a notable transformation. The contact is now, so to speak, less obvious than in the first two symphonies. The finale may be said to epitomize the general tendency of the work; it is an impressive ode to the courage and perseverance of man.

One day during the war Sibelius said: 'Civilization is strength and not weakness: those who believe the contrary are quite wrong. Look at the great nations of Europe and what they have endured! No savage could have stood the things that they have gone through. It is their civilization that has given them such moral strength and courage.' And he emphasized this idea by adding: 'I do believe in civilization.'

There can be no doubt about it: the events of the war strongly affected Sibelius. He told me that the idea he had just expressed had haunted his mind ever since the autumn of 1914. The perseverance and courage which Sibelius so greatly admired belong to the epic view of life. All the soldiers enduring the hardship of life in the trenches month after month, and facing death every day, were looking beyond the moment. Sibelius, the symphonist, was struck by the moral grandeur of this tragedy. It was about six months after the completion of his Fifth symphony that he spoke to me of the war; and, as we have seen, he had been haunted by this idea since 1914. His words must therefore show at least one part of the mental atmosphere in which he lived at the time when the Fifth symphony was conceived.

We must not, however, try to find any immediate references to the war in this work; for such would be fundamentally opposed to his principles. And, indeed, there are parts of the symphony, as for instance the famous slow movement, which would seem to indicate an entirely different origin. Yet all the preceding elements logically prepare the finale. The essence of this impressive movement is strength, energy, perseverance, an irresistible will, which gradually works itself up to an overpowering apotheosis in the last sonorous statement of its triumphant theme. A connection of some kind must exist between this conception and the gigantic contemporary drama enacted on the battlefields of Europe.

Sibelius' Fifth symphony plays in his mental evolution a part which is nearly analogous to that of the corresponding work in Beethoven's vast output, the C-minor Symphony. With the exception of his Fourth symphony, the Finnish composer so far follows the line of the master of Bonn. Like Beethoven he preserves undisturbed his broad symphonic outlook, although the intensity of his temperament would seem to make this impossible. Thus he remains in opposition to the essentially lyric and dramatic type of symphonic writing as represented by Schubert, Berlioz and Tchaikowsky.

Sibelius' Fifth symphony, his return to life, magnificently concludes a period in his creative activity. After the triumphant hymn of its finale the contemplative element becomes more and more prominent.

I have already quoted Sibelius saying that he considers Mozart and Mendelssohn the two greatest geniuses of the orchestra. These significant words date from the period after the completion of the Fifth symphony, or rather the first version of it; and they are supported by another contemporary statement of the master's. One day Sibelius told me: 'The older I grow, the more classical I become.' He developed the theme and then concluded: 'It is curious, you know: the more I see of life the more I feel convinced that classicism is the way of the future.' It must be remembered that this was said at a time when atonal music and extravagant experiments of every description dominated the concert-halls of Europe.

Once again we find that Sibelius has been as good as his word. His Sixth and Seventh symphonies are classical in the strictest sense of the term. They nobly continue the epic line of Haydn and Mozart, and are pre-Beethoven in spirit. In them we find the symphonic idea reduced to essentials. Nothing could be more illustrative of Sibelius' saying, that he considers a Mozart allegro the ideal model for a symphonic movement. These two works indeed realize the 'uninterrupted flowing' which commands his admiration in the symphonic movements of that youthful genius. And they have another quality in common with the symphonic masterpieces of Haydn and Mozart, an attitude of aloofness towards the exterior manifestations of life. The days are past and gone when the ardent temperament of Sibelius reacted to any impression. Contemplation, the essence of the age of wisdom, now dominates his outlook entirely.

Sibelius, the epic master, begins as an adherent of the type of symphonic writing inaugurated by Beethoven, though with a certain kinship to the romantic school as represented by Tchaikowsky. His Fourth symphony remains an isolated case in his own output, as it is in the history of music. After his Fifth symphony, he joins, in spirit, the line initiated by Haydn and Mozart. At every phase of his development he proves himself a true symphonist, his epic outlook being dominated by his deep psychological perspective. And although some of his seven monumental scores present certain affinities with types of symphonic writing already existing, all of them remain intensely personal to the signature of the greatest composer now living—Jean Sibelius.

VII

During one of my lessons Sibelius again attacked the problem of orchestration, this time from a quite different point of view. I had written an allegro passage, and I suggested that it should be played by the bass-clarinet. 'You must remember', he answered, 'that the bass-clarinet is an elderly gentleman; you mustn't ask him to run too fast!' He then gave very expressive and humorous characters to the different instruments and groups of instruments. Then, as an example of poetical atmosphere created by the simplest means, he mentioned the end of the pastorale in Berlioz' *Symphonie Fantastique*, where the whole musical picture is given by a pianissimo dialogue of two cors anglais accompanied by the kettle-drums. 'But sometimes', he added, 'Berlioz' fortissimo is brutal compared for instance to that of Tchaikowsky, which is never so, in spite of its dynamic intensity.'

He also discussed the orchestration of Bruckner.
'To Bruckner the orchestra was a huge organ,' he
said. 'Writing scores was for him like sitting in the
organ-loft of a church with all the keyboards in
reach. He simply used the different registers, without thinking of their instrumental individuality.
That is why he wrote flute passages for the horns, for
instance.' Sibelius concluded exactly as he had done
in discussing Brahms: Bruckner being a genius,
everything written by him was interesting in spite
of its clumsiness.

That day Sibelius emphasized the importance of
economizing one's resources. 'Think of Grieg writing his string quartette!' he said. 'He starts on a
chord using all the strings of the four instruments
in fortissimo. What possibilities will be left for the
rest of the work, if he begins with the biggest available climax?'

The subject of double chords induced him to give
me some important practical advice. He strongly
recommended me to use open strings for double
chords in my orchestral writing when opportunity
arose. There are many instances in Sibelius' own
work of a most skilful utilization of such opportuni-
ties. The beginning of the first statement of the
andante theme in the finale of the First symphony
gives us an especially fine example. (14) Here the

intense, sombre colour is made possible by the open C on the violoncellos.

Sibelius gave me yet another piece of technical advice. Many composers, so he told me, consider it a matter of minor importance how and when they interrupt instruments, whether a whole group of them or a part. To his mind it is a question to be considered most carefully, and by no means schematically. Sibelius' own highly interesting 'ceasing technique' is as a matter of fact one of the characteristic and original features of his scores. The opening bars of the Fourth symphony may be quoted in this connection. They begin with an expression of foreboding, whose echo seems to linger on the air. This very impressive image is created by the simplest means. The first subject is given out by the bassoons in unison with the muted and divided violoncellos and double-basses. At the end of the third bar the second bassoon stops, then at the end of the next bar the first bassoon stops, while the other instruments continue. Thus the impression of echo and listening is achieved. (15)

One day Sibelius spoke of composers, who have been spoilt by 'too good' orchestras. 'Take Mahler, for instance,' he said. 'He writes a fifth for a viola and a horn. I know perfectly well how he wants it to sound, but there are four or five orchestras in the whole world which could render it properly.'

Unlike so many musicians, Sibelius is deeply interested in literature, fine art, history and other subjects. He is opposed to the current fallacy which argues abstention from anything that might make one lose one's originality or individual character. Having himself a strong, vital personality he thinks it ridiculous to entertain such fears. On the contrary, he insists on the necessity of studying everything that will help to open one's eyes and broaden one's outlook. To him all this is a necessary complement to the creative activity of the composer. Many of his happiest and most popular inspirations have originated in his reading and contact with other arts. Only feeble individuals are afraid of these ever flowing sources of inspiration. Always when discussing this subject he comes back to the idea which he has so often expressed to me: 'I feel convinced that evolution is carried out by a very small number of individuals; the others only provide the material.'

Sibelius has therefore no sympathy for the crowd —as distinct from the people—and its tendency to encroach. Being a great individualist, he frankly confesses himself unable to tolerate stupid people, though his natural kindness will in most cases induce him to adopt quite a different attitude to-

92

wards them. 'There is something uncanny about a stupid fellow,' he once declared. 'He frightens me, but he impresses me. As a matter of fact he is monumental, because you feel that he is an absolute entity and that no power on earth will make him change his mind.' Often Sibelius' great sense of humour has helped him in such encounters.

'You will have to reckon with the stupidity of people more often than not,' he told me during one of my lessons, and asked me whether I thought of writing a concerto for the piano or the violin. I told him that it would interest me very much indeed, and he went on: 'When you do, you must not forget the incredible stupidity of most virtuosos—of course I don't mean the great and glorious exceptions. And bear this in mind not only in writing the solo passages, but also and perhaps still more in elaborating the purely orchestral parts of your score. I warn you especially against long preludes and interludes. And this refers particularly to violin concertos. Think of the poor public! What enjoyment can there be in watching a stolid man, and waiting for him to get busy with his Stradivarius or Guarnerius or whatever it be? I once heard Beethoven's Violin concerto played by [here he mentioned one of the most famous violinists of the end of the last century]. During the long prelude I was completely fascinated by his stupid looks and irresistibly attracted by the magic impression of an empty brain. But as soon as he started playing I became absorbed in Beethoven's music.'[1]

Sibelius considers artists, their eccentricities and pettinesses, with a humorous understanding. One day he said: 'It is so difficult to mix with artists! You must choose business men to talk to, because artists only talk of money.'

Sibelius' whole personality impresses one by its simplicity and evenness. At one of my lessons he told me how happy he was not to have been an infant prodigy. He quoted Busoni, bitterly complaining to him of his own precociousness, which had robbed him of his childhood. 'Believe me,' he continued, 'the impressions of childhood form our most precious inheritance in life. The more I live the more I come back to them, and they remain an inexhaustible source of inspiration.'

He went on to make some remarks on the mentality of young people. 'Be careful', he said, 'not to be spendthrift with the themes and musical ideas of your youth. They are the richest and best you will ever invent, and even if you cannot give them at

[1]It will be remembered that in Sibelius' own Violin concerto, after a brief quaver on the violins, the solo violin attacks the main subject at once.

once their definite shape, they will later on form the basis of some of your happiest conceptions.' He thereupon told me how many times he had proved this for himself, and gave *En Saga* as an example. He continued: 'In your old age you will look back on the ideas of your youth, and you will perhaps be fortunate enough to find some of them in your sketchbooks quite forgotten amongst many other notes, and never used. Then you will take them up and the ardour of your youth expressed in the themes themselves will be combined with the knowledge and experience acquired during a long musical career. Themes are the most precious property of a composer, and I personally don't see how a work could be built up without them.'

Another day he spoke of simplicity as the fundamental basis of all his aesthetic ideas. He told me that he had many years ago spent some time with Richard Strauss in Germany, where both were to conduct some of their compositions. One day the two composers went for a walk and Sibelius happened to mention some of Strauss' earlier works. 'Yes, that is all very well,' the German composer answered, 'but at that time I had not yet got into the habit of dividing the violins.' Strauss uttered these words as if in extenuation. Sibelius, on the contrary, divides the violins only when he thinks it necessary. He considers division of the strings as one of those effects that should be used very carefully if they are not to lose their expressiveness and force. In harmonization as well as in handling the palette of the orchestra he takes his stand on the greatest simplicity, and in his view most composers nowadays make far too abundant use of all the extraordinary possibilities afforded them by the modern orchestra. Once when we met in Paris he told me that he had recently been to several concerts of contemporary orchestral music. 'And do you know what I felt?' he asked me. 'I longed for unmuted trumpets and undivided and unmuted violins! These people seem to be afraid of anything that is immediately given to us; their interest is practically confined to the *recherché*.'

It is the northerner who reacts in this manner. And Sibelius' art is intensely northern, though he possesses the magic of evoking quite different atmospheres, as for instance in two of his suites, *Pelléas et Mélisande* and *Belshazzar*. Sibelius' art is formed principally on the life, the past and the landscape of his country, the subtle colours, heroic strength and endless melancholy of which he has conquered for the patrimony of music. Not only has he invoked the vast forests, innumerable lakes and islands; he also has an intense feeling for the archipelago fringing the Gulf of Finland.

One day I mentioned the impression which always takes hold of me when returning to Finland across the Baltic, the first forebodings of our country being given us by low, reddish granite rocks emerging from the pale blue sea, solitary islands of a hard, archaic beauty, inhabited by hundreds of white sea-gulls. And I concluded by saying that this landscape many centuries ago was the cradle of the Vikings. 'Yes,' Sibelius answered eagerly, and his eyes flashed, 'and when we see those granite rocks we know why we are able to treat the orchestra as we do!'

These words were spoken by the man who has himself created the Northern style of orchestration.

In Southern art dark colours only mean accents, whereas to Northern artists they are a matter of sensibility. The shadows on Caravaggio's canvases are completely lacking in life. They simply form cold, dead contrasts to the vivid parts of the compositions, which sparkle with life, colour and light. It was Rembrandt who first infused an intense life into the shadows and sombre parts of his canvases. And compared to the violent Italian *bravo* the solitary Dutch master is a Northerner.

Analogies can be found in the history of music. Debussy's dark colours are poor and surprisingly monotonous compared to the infinite variety and subtlety of his brighter tints. Wagner, however, on many occasions deliberately aims at creating a gloomy Northern atmosphere. The famous narration of Wotan in the *Walküre* represents his greatest effort to this end. Admirable though it is, it is still more instructive. The copious use of unusual bass instruments is rather obvious and the whole conception of the scene is more a brilliant piece of rhetoric than an inspired musical image. Moreover it is not the North proper, but the setting of prehistoric Central Europe, that Wagner represents with these somewhat self-conscious dark colours.

Russian music is famous for its gloomy tints. Yet these magnificent sombre colours are essentially different from those of the North, being conditioned by the Slav atmosphere of submission, despair and death. Grieg was the first to give the dreams and thoughts of the Northern races a proper musical expression; but his orchestral workmanship is too poor to be taken seriously into account.

With Sibelius' first scores the Northern orchestral style was suddenly created. In this spontaneous orchestral language there was no deliberate Wagnerian search for dark colours. Nothing could be more intensely vibrant with life and feeling than the shadows of this new, rich palette. The musical chiaroscuro of the North had been created overnight.

At every period of his development Sibelius gives exactly the same infinite care to the dark colours and all their various shades, as to the subtlest and most sonorous timbres of the orchestra. The writing for strings in the last part of his Seventh symphony affords a magnificent illustration. (16)

VIII

For some months I continued submitting my scores to Sibelius. Then one afternoon he read through my manuscript as usual, and suddenly declared that day's lesson to be the last. His words came as a shock. Seeing my surprise, he explained: 'I cannot teach you anything more. You can stand on your own legs now, and if I went on giving you advice, it would only do you harm.'

I had had the unique opportunity of being in touch with a man who at every moment gives one the impression of a great genius. But Sibelius has nothing of the rigidity which is peculiar to the characters of Corneille's and Racine's tragedies. He is more akin to Shakespeare's heroes, at the same time human, great and humorous. It is perhaps significant that he professes a particular admiration for *The Tempest*; and a survey of his works will show that

100

his evolution has been parallel to that of the great English poet. Like Shakespeare Sibelius has reached the soft harmonious atmosphere of *The Winter's Tale* after the great tragic period of *Hamlet* and *King Lear*.

There are certain matters concerning which he is very reticent, while in other respects he will tell one all about himself. Once I ventured to ask him whether he had favourites among his own works— 'Be sure I have,' he answered, 'but nobody will ever know which!' It might be pointed out in this connection that there is no composition of his which he talks of so often as his Fourth symphony.

On the other hand, he will disclose generous and interesting hints about his sources of inspiration. Here is one instance. On a cold day at the end of the autumn he went for a walk. The crimson of the setting sun was reflected in the wide surface of the lake outside his villa, and the calm mirror of water was framed by a border of thin, pale grey ice. A huge bird came flying from the north and alighted on the lake. It was a white swan, resting for a while on its long journey to southern climes. As the sun went down the transparent frame of ice gradually approached the solitary bird from either side. Sibelius watched the scene until nightfall. He then went home to compose one of his andantes.

I would like to finish with an anecdote, which Sibelius told one day. He had been invited by a rich philanthropist and his wife to stay with them and was told beforehand that his host and hostess profoundly regretted not having any children. One day they asked their guest whether he had any children himself. Sibelius thought that he might hurt their feelings by frankly telling them that he had five daughters, and he therefore replied: 'No, I have no children.' With an increasing feeling of uneasiness he now discovered that his amiable host wished to know all about his people. He tried to answer as diplomatically as possible, but suddenly forgetting the part he had assumed, he happened to mention his eldest daughter. There came a moment of silent surprise, whereupon Sibelius was politely requested by his hostess to tell her something about his only daughter. This he did, and after a while he compared her to her younger sister. The philanthropist and his wife exchanged a glance, not knowing what to make of this. Their celebrated guest then gave them a look of awful concern and humbly confessed that he had still three more daughters.

This story may strike my readers as irrelevant; but I have told it because it paints the man.

I shall be well content if with these recollections

and anecdotes I have been able to trace a faint
picture of the man whom by exceptional privilege
I was fortunate enough to approach and whose work
is the meridian of contemporary music.

APPENDIX

(1) Symphony No 6; page 5

By permission of Wilhelm Hansen, Copenhagen and Leipzig. Proprietor for all countries.

Allegro molto moderato

The coincidence of the notes C and C♯ is softened, as they are given out by instruments of entirely different timbres.

(2) The Swan of Tuonela; page 4

By permission of Messrs Breitkopf and Härtel, Leipzig.
Proprietors for all countries.

Andante molto sostenuto

Pedal effect.

(3) Tapiola; page 3

By permission of Messrs Breitkopf and Härtel, Leipzig.
Proprietors for all countries.

Largamente

Pedal effect.

(4) Symphony No. 1; pages 44-45

By permission of Messrs Breitkopf and Härtel, Leipzig.
Proprietors for all countries.

Allegro energico

The colours of the trombones and of the tuba are reconciled by the quaver on the kettle-drums.

(5) Tapiola; page 60

By permission of Messrs Breitkopf and Härtel, Leipzig. Proprietors for all countries.

Allegro moderato

A fortissimo without a tuba.

(6) Symphony No. 2; page 142

By permission of Messrs Breitkopf and Härtel, Leipzig. Proprietors for all countries.

Allegro moderato

An exceptional case: the unity of the trombone trio is broken.

(7) Symphony No. 1; page 45

Allegro energico

Homophonous writing for the trombones in an earlier work.

(8) Symphony No. 7; page 9

Adagio

Polyphonic writing for the trombones in a later work.

(9) Symphony No. 1; pages 142-143

*By permission of Messrs Breitkopf and Härtel, Leipzig.
Proprietors for all countries.*

Andante (ma non troppo)

Fascinating dark colour obtained by the oboes and clarinets in the lower register.

(10) Tapiola; page 40

Allegro moderato

Curious effect obtained by unusual writing for the horns.

(11) *Brief formal analysis of the finale of the Second symphony*

The beginning of the first subject is given out by the strings (page 99):

(*a*) *Allegro moderato*

A climax is reached in the first statement of the entire theme (pages 103-104) for full orchestra:

(*b*)

The first subject (*Hauptsatz*) finishes on the first chord of the 44th bar at letter B of the score (page 105). It is immediately followed by the transition (*Übergangssatz*), the theme of which is given by the wood-wind:

(*c*)

The transition contains 22 bars.

The second subject (*Seitensatz*) begins at letter C (page 107). Whereas the initial key was D-major we are now in f-sharp-minor. The accompanying figure starts on the violoncellos:

(*d*)

The theme itself is presented under various forms, such as:

(*e*)

and:

(f)

There are 36 bars in the second subject. The first chord of the 37th bar, which ends this episode, also introduces the conclusion (page 111, second bar). The theme of the conclusion (*Schluss-satz*) is given out by the two first trombones:

(g)

After these four bars the theme assumes the character of a coda, which begins at letter D (page 112, *moderato assai*):

(h)

These seven bars end the first part of the finale.

The second part is formed by the 'working out.' It starts at once (*a tempo ma tranquillo*, page 112) and

113

contains 84 bars. The themes exemplified by (*a*), (*e*), (*h*), (*f*) are here elaborated.

The third part starts at letter K (page 120). It corresponds exactly to the first part except that this time the second subject is given in d-minor according to the classical rules. This part contains 151 bars (it finishes on page 142).

The big coda—not to be confused with the small coda following the conclusion (*Schluss-satz*)—begins at letter S (page 143). This coda, the 'second working out', is short and consequently entirely different from the gigantic codas characteristic of many of Beethoven's works. The whole finale is built up like a Mozart allegro.

(12) Symphony No. 7; page 73

By permission of Wilhelm Hansen, Copenhagen and Leipzig. Proprietor for all countries.

Adagio

It is at present not possible to bring out a crescendo or a fortissimo in the lower register of the trombones. This passage and the one that follows require a further development of instrumental and mechanical technique before the intentions of the composer can be satisfactorily rendered.

114

(13) Symphony No. 6; page 10

Allegro molto moderato

Neither the piano pianissimo nor the modulations are really possible in the lower register of the bassoons.

(14) Symphony No. 1; page 118

Andante assai

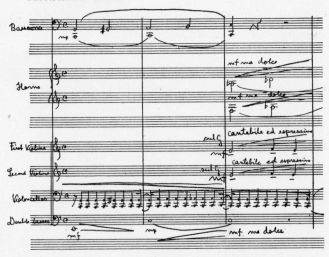

Striking colour obtained by the utilization of the open C for the double chords on the violoncellos.

115

(15) Symphony No. 4; page 1

By permission of Messrs Breitkopf and Härtel, Leipzig.
Proprietors for all countries.

Tempo molto moderato, quasi adagio

The bassoons are interrupted, while the violoncellos and double basses continue. An effect of echoing and listening is thus obtained.

(16) Symphony No. 7; pages 65-66

By permission of Wilhelm Hansen, Copenhagen and Leipzig. Proprietor for all countries.

Presto

Striking and original colour obtained by the division of the lower strings.